GARFIELD MEETS THE PRESIDENTS!

Facts, Stats, and Totally True Trivia on every U.S. President

CREATED BY
JIM DAVIS

SCHOLASTIC INC.

New York   Toronto   London   Auckland   Sydney

Mexico City   New Delhi   Hong Kong   Buenos Aires

ISBN 0-439-69001-3

All rights reserved. Published by Scholastic Inc. © 2004 PAWS

SCHOLASTIC and associated logos are trademarks and/or registered trademarks of Scholastic Inc.

12 11 10 9 8 7 6 5 4 3 2 1   4 5 6 7 8 9

Printed in the U.S.A.

First printing, October 2004

Designed by Rocco Melillo   •   Cover design by Louise Bova

Hello, history buffs and feline fans! Garfield here. I'm here to tell you about the presidents of the United States.

The president can seem larger than life. He lives in a big house. He always has a bunch of people around him. Plus, he's on television a lot (interrupting my favorite TV shows, I might add).

This book is not your ordinary history book. You'll discover little-known facts, colorful habits, and (best of all) favorite foods of the U.S. presidents. That's right! I'll let you know which president barked like a dog, which one got stuck in his bathtub, and which one had phones installed everywhere (even in the pool).

Sounds a bit odd?

Maybe things would be different if a cat were president. Hmmm . . . I'll think about that while you read.

Before you get started, here are some presidential terms you'll come across in this book.

Address - This doesn't always mean where someone lives. An address is a speech the president gives.

Aide - An assistant to the president.

Cabinet - This could be a place to keep dishes, but the president's cabinet is a group of advisors and department heads.

First Family - A name for the president's family.

First Lady - She is, you guessed it, the president's wife.

Impeach - If a president goes on trial before Congress, he is impeached.

Inauguration - The formal ceremony beginning the president's term in office.

Party - This doesn't always mean a fun get-together with plenty of food (as great as that sounds). A *political* party is a group of people who believe in the same political ideas. Some party names are: Democratic, Federalist, Republican, and Whig.

Term - The amount of time a president stays in office.

Veto - If a president doesn't like a bill and doesn't want to make it a law by signing it, he or she vetoes it.

White House - The house where the president and the First Family live. It's in Washington, D.C.

George Washington

PRESIDENT NUMBER: I
YEARS HE WAS PRESIDENT: 1789-1797
FIRST LADY: MARTHA WASHINGTON

The old story about George Washington chopping down his father's cherry tree is not really true. It was written in a book by Parson Mason Weems. This writer wanted to create inspiring legends for the new country.

Washington was often credited with the development of the mule. A mule is the offspring of a donkey and a horse.

Washington didn't really have wooden false teeth. Instead, he had dentures made from gold, lead, and ivory. He even had one set made from hippopotamus teeth.

He was the first president to appear on a postage stamp.

He thought regular bathing was unhealthy.

He wore size 13 shoes!

George Washington has one state, seven mountains, eight streams, ten lakes, thirty-three counties, and 121 towns and villages named after him.

> I CANNOT TELL A LIE. IT WAS I WHO ATE THOSE TWELVE LASAGNAS

FUN FACTS

Nickname: Father of His Country
Occupations before being president: surveyor, farmer, soldier
Favorite foods: ice cream, fish (preferably not at the same time)
Hobbies or sports: fishing, horseback riding
Pets: a horse named Nelson; four dogs named Sweet Lips, Vulcan, Madame Moose, and True Love; other dogs and horses

WHAT WAS HAPPENING:

• The French Revolution ended the monarchy in France.
• The Bill of Rights became law.
• The U.S. population was about 4,900,000.
• There were only thirteen stars on our flag.

John Adams

PRESIDENT NUMBER: 2
YEARS HE WAS PRESIDENT: 1797-1801
FIRST LADY: ABIGAIL ADAMS

Adams was the first president to live in the White House. He moved in while it was still being built. Wet plaster oozed from the walls, the bathrooms were outdoors, and the main source of water was at a park five blocks away.

He was the first president to be the father of another president—John Quincy Adams.

He established our country's naval department.

John Adams once swiped a sliver of wood from a chair at William Shakespeare's birthplace.

KEEPETH THE SLIVER, I'LL HAVETH A BURGER

FUN FACTS

Nickname: Duke of Braintree
Occupations before being president: teacher, lawyer, congressional delegate, diplomat, vice president
Favorite foods: cider, white potatoes, cranberries, ham
Hobbies or sports: reading, horseback riding, collecting souvenirs
Pets: a horse named Cleopatra, dogs

WHAT WAS HAPPENING:

- Napoleon became dictator of France.
- The Department of the Navy was formed.
- The U.S. population was about 4,900,000.
- There were fifteen stars on the flag.

Thomas Jefferson

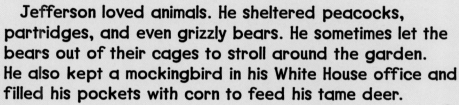

PRESIDENT NUMBER: 3

YEARS HE WAS PRESIDENT: 1801-1809

FIRST LADY: MARTHA JEFFERSON

(SHE DIED BEFORE HE BECAME PRESIDENT; HIS DAUGHTER, MARTHA, ACTED AS HOSTESS AT THE WHITE HOUSE.)

AN ICE-COLD FOOT BATH A DAY . . .

Jefferson loved animals. He sheltered peacocks, partridges, and even grizzly bears. He sometimes let the bears out of their cages to stroll around the garden. He also kept a mockingbird in his White House office and filled his pockets with corn to feed his tame deer.

He bathed his feet daily in ice-cold water. He believed this would prevent colds.

His grandson was the first baby born in the White House.

Thomas Jefferson sold his collection of 6,500 books to the United States to establish the Library of Congress. It took eleven wagons to transport all the books.

BOOKS ARE GOOD BRAIN FOOD

Beauty and the Feast

WAR & PIZZA

THE THREE MUNCHKETEERS

FUN FACTS

Nickname: Red Fox

Occupations before being president: lawyer, farmer, architect, legislator, governor, congressman, foreign minister, secretary of state, vice president

Favorite foods: ice cream, pancakes, fresh asparagus

Hobbies or sports: fishing, running, playing the violin

Pets: birds

WHAT WAS HAPPENING:

- The United States purchased the Louisiana Territory from France.
- The U.S. population was about 7,040,000.
- There were fifteen stars on the flag.

James Madison

PRESIDENT NUMBER: 4
YEARS HE WAS PRESIDENT: 1809-1817
FIRST LADY: DOLLEY MADISON

YOU MUST BE AT LEAST THIS TALL TO BE THE PRESIDENT

Madison was the smallest president—five feet six inches tall and weighing just over a hundred pounds.

Dolley Madison was the first First Lady to serve ice cream at the White House.

During the War of 1812, the British army was closing in on Washington, D.C. Before leaving the White House, Dolley Madison packed up the Declaration of Independence, the national seal, a portrait of George Washington, and their pet parrot.

IT'S ABOUT TIME!

Madison was the only person taking notes when the Constitution was written, giving us the only record of the process.

FASHION ALERT: Madison was the first president to wear regular trousers instead of "knee breeches."

FUN FACTS

Nickname: Father of the Constitution
Occupations before being president: legislator, secretary of state
Favorite foods: ice cream, chocolate
Sports or hobbies: horseback riding
Pets: a parrot

WHAT WAS HAPPENING:

- The War of 1812 began.
- Francis Scott Key wrote "The Star-Spangled Banner."
- The U.S. population was about 8,900,000.
- There were fifteen stars on the flag.

James Monroe

PRESIDENT NUMBER: 5
YEARS HE WAS PRESIDENT: 1817-1825
FIRST LADY: ELIZABETH MONROE

NO MORE COLONIES, THANKS. WE'RE FULL

Monroe's daughter was the first to be married in the White House.

He was the last president to have served as an officer in the Revolutionary War and was the only one wounded.

He proclaimed the Monroe Doctrine, which warned European nations against establishing any more colonies in the Americas.

Monroe was the first president to tour the country.

HMMM . . . WHILE HE'S GONE . . . I THINK I'LL TOUR THE KITCHEN

wig.

FUN FACTS

Nickname: Last of the Cocked Hats
Occupations before being president: soldier, lawyer, senator, diplomat, governor, secretary of state, secretary of war
Pets: a spaniel

WHAT WAS HAPPENING:

- The first public high school was opened.
- Washington Irving wrote the short story "Rip Van Winkle."
- The U.S. population was about 11,300,000.
- There were fifteen stars on the flag.

John Quincy Adams

PRESIDENT NUMBER: 6
YEARS HE WAS PRESIDENT: 1825-1829
FIRST LADY: LOUISA JOHNSON ADAMS

His father was the second president—John Adams.

Adams was the first president to install a pool table in the White House.

He was the only president to name a son George Washington.

Adams liked to skinny-dip in the Potomac River behind the White House.

He published a book of poetry and he could speak four languages.

FASHION ALERT: Adams wore the same hat every day for ten years.

LASAGNA . . . HOW DO I LOVE THEE? LET ME COUNT THE WAYS. . . .

UH . . . WRONG KIND OF POOL

FUN FACTS

Nickname: Old Man Eloquent
Occupations before being president: lawyer, writer, diplomat, senator, secretary of state
Hobbies or sports: billiards, swimming, walking
Pets: silkworms, an alligator

WHAT WAS HAPPENING:

- Webster's dictionary was first published.
- The first passenger railroad in America began laying track.
- The U.S. population was about 11,252,237.
- There were twenty-four stars on the flag.

Andrew Jackson

PRESIDENT NUMBER: 7
YEARS HE WAS PRESIDENT: 1829-1837
FIRST LADY: RACHEL JACKSON (SHE DIED BEFORE HE TOOK OFFICE.)

Jackson was the first president to ride a train.

He was the first president to be born in a log cabin.

He was the only president to have been a prisoner of war in the Revolutionary War.

Jackson added running water and fully equipped bathrooms to the White House.

The Creek Indians called him "Sharp Knife."

ALL ABOARD!

I CALL ODIE "DULL MIND"

FUN FACTS

Nickname: Old Hickory
Occupations before being president: soldier, lawyer, senator, judge
Favorite foods: pancakes
Hobbies or sports: horseback riding, breeding racehorses
Pets: horses, a parrot named Poll

WHAT WAS HAPPENING:

- The Democratic Party met for the first time.
- Texas declared independence from Mexico during the Battle of the Alamo.
- The U.S. population was about 15,900,000.
- There were twenty-four stars on the flag.

Martin Van Buren

PRESIDENT NUMBER: 8
YEARS HE WAS PRESIDENT: 1837-1841
FIRST LADY: HANNAH VAN BUREN (SHE DIED BEFORE HE BECAME PRESIDENT.)

He was the first president born in America after it had become the United States and was no longer a British colony.

HE WAS OK IN MY BOOK!

He was often criticized for the fine clothes he wore and his expensive tastes.

Because his nickname was "Old Kinderhook," a Democratic Party organization formed in his honor was called the O.K. Club. They used "OK" as their slogan, and we still use the term today.

His other nickname was "Little Magician."

PRESTO! A GOOFBALL!

FUN FACTS

Nickname: Old Kinderhook, Little Magician
Occupations before being president: lawyer, state attorney general, senator, secretary of state, vice president
Hobbies or sports: horseback riding, fishing
Pets: two tiger cubs

WHAT WAS HAPPENING:

- Goodyear discovered how to vulcanize rubber.
- England issued the world's first postage stamp.
- The U.S. population was about 17,700,000.
- There were twenty-five stars on the flag.

William Henry Harrison

I PRESCRIBE A NICE PAN OF LASAGNA FOR MYSELF

PRESIDENT NUMBER: 9
YEAR HE WAS PRESIDENT: 1841
FIRST LADY: ANNA HARRISON

He was the only president to have attended medical school.

At sixty-eight, he was the oldest man to become president at that time.

He was the only president to have a grandson become president—Benjamin Harrison.

NO PNEUMONIA FOR US. WE'RE WEARING GLOVES BEHIND OUR BACKS

Once elected, Harrison gave the longest inauguration speech in history, on a frosty day, without an overcoat, hat, or gloves. He came down with pneumonia and died after only one month in office. That made him the first president to die in office.

FUN FACTS

Nickname: Old Tippecanoe
Occupations before being president: army officer, congressman, governor, senator, diplomat
Pets: a goat and a cow

WHAT WAS HAPPENING:

- The U.S. population was about 17,700,000.
- There were twenty-six stars on the flag.

John Tyler

PRESIDENT NUMBER: 10
YEARS HE WAS PRESIDENT: 1841-1845
FIRST LADY: LETITIA TYLER (SHE DIED
DURING HIS PRESIDENCY); JULIA TYLER

Tyler was the first vice president to inherit the presidency after a president died in office.

He was the first president to have a veto overridden.

Tyler and his wife danced the polka in the White House.

He had fifteen children, making him the president with the most children.

THAT'S A BIG LITTER!

IT'S NOT THE POLKA, BUT IT'S A LOT OF FUN!

FUN FACTS

Nickname: His Accidency

Occupations before being president: lawyer, congressman, governor, senator, vice president

Hobbies or sports: playing the violin

Pets: a horse named General, a greyhound named Le Beau, two Italian wolfhounds

WHAT WAS HAPPENING:

- Samuel Morse demonstrated his electric telegraph before Congress.
- Kit Carson and John C. Frémont explored the western United States, including California.
- The U.S. population was about 20,200,000.
- There were twenty-six stars on the flag.

James K. Polk

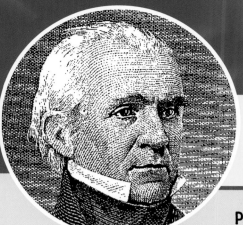

PRESIDENT NUMBER: 11
YEARS HE WAS PRESIDENT: 1845-1849
FIRST LADY: SARAH POLK

Polk didn't trust banks. He kept his money in bags hidden around the house.

He was the first president to have his inauguration reported by telegraph.

Polk decided to serve only one term as president, even though he could have easily won another election.

NEWS

ONE WORD . . . BORING!

No music, cards, or dancing were allowed at his White House parties because of Sarah Polk's religious beliefs.

FUN FACTS

Nickname: Young Hickory
Occupations before being president: lawyer, congressman, governor
Pets: none

WHAT WAS HAPPENING:

- The sewing machine was patented.
- The first U.S. postage stamps were issued.
- Gold was discovered in California.
- The U.S. population was about 22,700,000.
- There were twenty-six stars on the flag.

Zachary Taylor

PRESIDENT NUMBER: 12
YEARS HE WAS PRESIDENT: 1849-1850
FIRST LADY: MARGARET TAYLOR

Taylor rode his horse sidesaddle into battle. It was the way ladies generally rode horses.

He was the first president who had never held a previous political office.

After just sixteen months in office, he suffered severe cramps after eating pickled cucumbers, cherries, and milk. He died five days later. Doctors believed that either the cherries or the milk were contaminated.

I RIDE DOG-SADDLE!

OKAY, FOR THE FIRST TIME, I'M NOT HUNGRY

FUN FACTS

Nickname: Old Rough and Ready
Occupations before being president: army officer, plantation owner
Hobbies or sports: horseback riding
Pets: a horse named Old Whitey

WHAT WAS HAPPENING:

- The California gold rush began.
- The Department of the Interior was created.
- The U.S. population was about 23,300,000.
- There were thirty stars on the flag.

Millard Fillmore

PRESIDENT NUMBER: 13
YEARS HE WAS PRESIDENT: 1850–1853
FIRST LADY: ABIGAIL FILLMORE

Fillmore was the first president with a stepmother.

He and his wife switched from cooking on an open fireplace to a stove (although no one in the White House, including the cook, knew how to use it at first).

Abigail was the first First Lady to have held a job outside the home. She was a teacher.

Actually, she was Fillmore's teacher when he was nineteen!

Fillmore and his wife established the first permanent library for First Families in the White House.

DOES THIS LIBRARY COME WITH A REMOTE?

FUN FACTS

Nickname: Last of the Whigs
Occupations before being president: lawyer, congressman, vice president
Pets: none

WHAT WAS HAPPENING:

- Henri Giffard flew the first successful airship.
- Direct rail service began between New York City and Chicago.
- The U.S. population was about 25,700,000.
- There were thirty stars on the flag.

Franklin Pierce

PRESIDENT NUMBER: 14
YEARS HE WAS PRESIDENT: 1853-1857
FIRST LADY: JANE PIERCE

Pierce had the first Christmas tree in the White House.

He installed central heating and a second bathroom in the White House.

He always insisted that grace be said before every meal.

Pierce was the only president to keep everyone in his cabinet during his entire term in office. No one left or was fired.

He was old friends with famous author Nathaniel Hawthorne.

While fighting in the Mexican War, Pierce fainted and fell off his horse—twice.

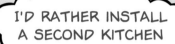

I'D RATHER INSTALL A SECOND KITCHEN

I SOMETIMES FAINT AFTER A NICE, HEFTY SNACK

FUN FACTS

Nickname: Handsome Frank
Occupations before being president: lawyer, congressman, senator, army officer
Pets: none

WHAT WAS HAPPENING:

- The Republican Party was formed.
- About 400,000 immigrants arrived in New York City.
- The U.S. population was about 29,000,000.
- There were thirty-one stars on the flag.

James Buchanan

PRESIDENT NUMBER: 15
YEARS HE WAS PRESIDENT: 1857-1861
FIRST LADY: NONE

Buchanan served twelve hundred gallons of ice cream to guests at his inauguration.

He was the first and only bachelor president. Harriet Lane, his niece, served as the official White House hostess.

Because he wasn't married, people sent him pets for company. Some animals in his "zoo" were a herd of elephants, a pair of bald eagles, and a Newfoundland dog.

NOW THAT'S A COOL PARTY!

Buchanan was nearsighted in one eye and farsighted in the other. He compensated by cocking his head to the left.

I DON'T READ EYE CHARTS. I READ PIE CHARTS

FUN FACTS

Nickname: Ten-Cent Jimmy
Occupations before being president: lawyer, soldier, congressman, diplomat, senator, secretary of state
Favorite foods: cabbage
Pets: a Newfoundland named Lara, bald eagles, a herd of elephants

WHAT WAS HAPPENING:

- The Pony Express showed that mail could be delivered promptly across the American West.
- The Confederate states began to organize in hopes of seceding from the Union.
- The U.S. population was about 32,400,000.
- There were thirty-one stars on the flag.

Abraham Lincoln

PRESIDENT NUMBER: 16
YEARS HE WAS PRESIDENT: 1861-1865
FIRST LADY: MARY TODD LINCOLN

Lincoln was the tallest president at six feet four inches.

He established Thanksgiving Day.

I KEEP SNACKS IN MINE

He signed the Emancipation Proclamation, which freed the slaves, and he used to keep important papers in his famous stovepipe hat.

Mrs. Lincoln owned more than five hundred pairs of gloves.

AND WE'RE ALL VERY, VERY THANKFUL!

© PAWS

Lincoln's presidency came to a tragic end in 1865. While attending a play at the Ford Theatre, he was shot by an actor named John Wilkes Booth and died shortly thereafter.

Lincoln is the only president to have his likeness on both sides of a coin. His profile is on the penny. But if you take a magnifying glass and examine the back, you'll see him sitting inside the Lincoln Memorial.

FUN FACTS

Nickname: Honest Abe
Occupations before being president: laborer, store clerk, soldier, lawyer, state legislator, congressman
Favorite foods: fruit salad, cheese, oysters, fricasseed chicken
Pets: a horse, ponies, two goats named Nanko and Nanny, a pig, a rabbit, cats, dogs

WHAT WAS HAPPENING:

- The Civil War raged for four years.
- The first paper money was issued by the government of the United States.
- The U.S. population was about 32,351,000.
- There were thirty-three stars on the flag.

Andrew Johnson

PRESIDENT NUMBER: 17
YEARS HE WAS PRESIDENT: 1865-1869
FIRST LADY: ELIZA JOHNSON

Johnson's wife taught him to read and write.

Being a former tailor, Johnson made all his own clothing.

Johnson was the first president to be impeached.

He would not get rid of mice; he would leave out flour and water for them instead.

FUN FACTS

Nickname: Tennessee Tailor

Occupations before being president: tailor, mayor, congressman, governor, senator, vice president

Favorite foods: fish, jam

Hobbies or sports: gardening, playing checkers

Pets: mice

WHAT WAS HAPPENING:

- Alaska was purchased from Russia.
- The first practical typewriter was patented.
- Alfred Nobel of Sweden invented dynamite.
- The U.S. population was about 39,100,000.
- There were thirty-five stars on the flag.

Ulysses S. Grant

PRESIDENT NUMBER: 18
YEARS HE WAS PRESIDENT: 1869-1877
FIRST LADY: JULIA GRANT

Grant was the commander of the Union Army during the Civil War.

He was the first president to have a woman run against him during a campaign—Victoria Woodhull.

He thought it was bad luck to retrace one's steps.

I THINK IT'S BAD LUCK TO SKIP A MEAL

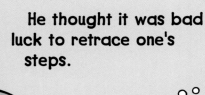

SLOW DOWN, PAL!

Grant was the only president to receive a speeding ticket while riding a horse!

FUN FACTS

Nickname: Uncle Sam, Unconditional Surrender

Occupations before being president: farmer, clerk, army officer

Favorite foods: cucumbers soaked in vinegar

Hobbies or sports: swimming

Pets: dogs, horses, birds

WHAT WAS HAPPENING:

- Alexander Graham Bell invented the telephone.
- The Yellowstone area was set aside as the first national park.
- The U.S. population was about 47,141,000.
- There were thirty-seven stars on the flag.

Rutherford B. Hayes

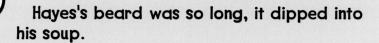

PRESIDENT NUMBER: 19
YEARS HE WAS PRESIDENT: 1877-1881
FIRST LADY: LUCY HAYES

WHAT A GREAT IDEA! HE COULD SAVE SOME FOR LATER

Hayes's beard was so long, it dipped into his soup.

Mrs. Hayes became one of the first people to talk on a telephone when Alexander Graham Bell (inventor of the telephone) and his assistant brought their invention to the White House.

Mrs. Hayes started the White House Easter egg roll.

FUN FACTS

Nickname: His Fraudulency

Occupations before being president: lawyer, army officer, congressman, governor

Hobbies or sports: croquet, shooting

Pets: the first Siamese kitten in America, dogs, cows, horses, a goat, canaries

WHAT WAS HAPPENING:

- Cleveland, Ohio, became the first American city to install electric streetlights.
- Thomas Edison invented the phonograph.
- The U.S. population was about 51,500,000.
- There were thirty-seven stars on the flag.

23

James A. Garfield

PRESIDENT NUMBER: 20
YEAR HE WAS PRESIDENT: 1881
FIRST LADY: LUCRETIA GARFIELD

James Garfield did not serve a long term as president. Less than a year after his inauguration, he was assassinated.

When he was sixteen, Garfield tried to run away to sea. He was turned down, but he did sign on to a canal boat that sailed from Cleveland to Pittsburgh.

He was the first left-handed president.

He was the first president to campaign in English and Spanish.

Sometimes, to entertain his friends, James Garfield would write a Greek sentence with his right hand, write a Latin sentence with his left, and speak German at the same time.

He sometimes greeted people by barking like a dog.

He juggled clubs to build up his muscles.

I'LL RUN AWAY TO SEA, BUT ONLY IF THE FISHING IS GOOD

SS Garfield

FUN FACTS

Nickname: Preacher President
Occupations before being president: teacher, preacher, professor, college president, army officer, congressman
Hobbies or sports: billiards, playing cards, reading
Pets: a dog named Veto, a mare

WHAT WAS HAPPENING:

- The American Red Cross was organized.
- The last big cattle drive from Texas to Kansas took place.
- The U.S. population was about 51,500,000.
- There were thirty-eight stars on the flag.

Chester A. Arthur

PRESIDENT NUMBER: 21
YEARS HE WAS PRESIDENT: 1881-1885
FIRST LADY: ELLEN ARTHUR (SHE DIED BEFORE HE BECAME PRESIDENT.)

As a young student, Arthur once dumped the school bell into the Erie Canal.

Not happy with the old furniture in the White House, he organized a huge lawn sale and sold the furniture for more than eight thousand dollars.

Arthur owned more than two hundred pairs of pants. That came in handy because he changed his pants several times a day.

FOR SALE ONE DOG SLIGHTLY SILLY

PANTS ARE OVERRATED

FUN FACTS

Nickname: Elegant Arthur

Occupations before being president: teacher, lawyer, New York militia, inspector general, custom house collector, vice president

Favorite food: muttonchops

Hobbies or sports: fishing, long walks

WHAT WAS HAPPENING:

- The Brooklyn Bridge was completed.
- German immigrant Anton Feuchtwanger invented the hot dog.
- The gunfight at the O.K. Corral took place in Tombstone, Arizona.
- The U.S. population was about 51,500,000.
- There were thirty-eight stars on the flag.

Grover Cleveland

PRESIDENT NUMBER: 22
YEARS HE WAS PRESIDENT: 1885-1889
FIRST LADY: FRANCES CLEVELAND

Cleveland was the only president to get married in the White House.

At twenty-one, Frances Cleveland was the youngest First Lady.

He was the only president to have a child born in the White House, a baby girl named Esther.

A BOUNCING BABY . . . GIRL!

FUN FACTS

Nickname: Uncle Jumbo, Old Veto
Occupations before being president: lawyer, sheriff, mayor, governor
Hobbies or sports: fishing
Pets: birds, a poodle

WHAT WAS HAPPENING:

- The Statue of Liberty, a gift from France, was dedicated in New York City.
- John Pemberton invented Coca-Cola.
- The U.S. population was about 61,800,000.
- There were thirty-eight stars on the flag.

Benjamin Harrison

PRESIDENT NUMBER: 23
YEARS HE WAS PRESIDENT: 1889-1893
FIRST LADY: CAROLINE HARRISON

Harrison ordered that the U.S. flag be flown above the White House and other government buildings, including schools.

His grandfather was president William Henry Harrison.

Caroline Harrison was an artist.

Harrison was the first president to use electric lights in the White House. However, they were too afraid of shocks to ever turn them off.

WE'RE NOT SCARED. HIT THE SWITCH!

FUN FACTS

Nickname: Little Ben
Occupations before being president: lawyer, army officer, senator
Hobbies or sports: hunting
Pets: a goat, dogs

WHAT WAS HAPPENING:

• The Eiffel Tower was erected in Paris.
• The zipper was invented.
• Basketball was originated by James A. Naismith.
• The U.S. population was about 67,000,000.
• There were thirty-eight stars on the flag.

Grover Cleveland (again!)

PRESIDENT NUMBER: 24
YEARS HE WAS PRESIDENT: 1893-1897
FIRST LADY: FRANCES CLEVELAND

ONE MORE TIME!

He became the first and only president to serve two nonconsecutive terms.

He vetoed more bills than any president before him, earning the nickname "Old Veto."

AND HALLOWEEN WAS NEVER THE SAME AGAIN!

The candy bar Baby Ruth was named after his daughter.

FUN FACTS	WHAT WAS HAPPENING:
Nickname: Uncle Jumbo, Old Veto	Wilhelm Roentgen of Germany discovered X-rays.
Occupations before being president: lawyer, sheriff, mayor, governor	Henry Ford's first car was manufactured.
	The first lie-detector test was developed.
Hobbies or sports: fishing	The U.S. population was about 72,200,000.
Pets: birds, a poodle	There were forty-four stars on the flag.

William McKinley

PRESIDENT NUMBER: 25
YEARS HE WAS PRESIDENT: 1897-1901
FIRST LADY: IDA MCKINLEY

As a child, McKinley enjoyed building and flying kites.

To create a more serious mood, McKinley and his wife banned the color yellow from the White House.

He could greet and shake the hands of thirty people a minute.

He wore a red carnation in his lapel every day for good luck.

I CAN SHAKE SALT AND PEPPER OVER THIRTY MEATBALLS A MINUTE

I SPORT A FULL STOMACH EVERY DAY FOR GOOD LUCK

FUN FACTS

Nickname: Wobbly Willie
Occupations before being president: county prosecutor, army officer, congressman, governor
Hobbies or sports: horseback riding, swimming, walking
Pets: a Mexican double-yellow-headed parrot

WHAT WAS HAPPENING:

- The Spanish-American War began, lasting only a few months.
- The American Baseball League was organized.
- Hawaii, Guam, Puerto Rico, and the Philippines became American possessions.
- The U.S. population was about 77,600,000.
- There were forty-five stars on the flag.

29

Theodore Roosevelt

PRESIDENT NUMBER: 26
YEARS HE WAS PRESIDENT: 1901–1909
FIRST LADY: EDITH ROOSEVELT

While visiting family friends the Maxwells, Roosevelt finished his cup of coffee and said, "Good to the last drop." The Maxwell family sold their Maxwell House brand of coffee to General Foods and used that now famous slogan.

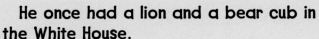

EVEN BETTER WITH A DOUGHNUT!

I'D BE FIRST TO SLEEP IN THE WHITE HOUSE KITCHEN

He once had a lion and a bear cub in the White House.

He was a champion boxer in college.

He often played hide-and-seek with his children in the White House attic. He always wanted to be "it."

On a hunt, he refused to shoot a bear cub. This act of kindness was the beginning of the name "teddy bear."

Roosevelt was the first president to ride in a car, fly in an airplane, and descend in a submarine.

FUN FACTS

Nickname: TR, Teddy
Occupations before being president: writer, state legislator, rancher, police commissioner, assistant secretary of the navy, cavalry commander, governor, vice president
Hobbies or sports: boxing, hunting, jujitsu, horseback riding, shooting, tennis, wrestling

WHAT WAS HAPPENING:

- The first wireless telegraph message was sent across the Atlantic Ocean.
- The Wright brothers made the first airplane flight.
- The first "Model T" Ford went on the market.
- The U.S. population was about 90,000,000.
- There were forty-five stars on the flag.

William Howard Taft

PRESIDENT NUMBER: 27
YEARS HE WAS PRESIDENT: 1909-1913
FIRST LADY: HELEN TAFT

THANK YOU, MR. PRESIDENT

Taft was the largest president, weighing in at 332 pounds.

He once learned to surf in Waikiki, Hawaii.

He was the first president to throw out the opening ball for a baseball season.

He was the first president to play golf.

Taft had a special bathtub built in the White House because he often got stuck in a normal-sized one and had to be pulled out.

NOT FUNNY

FUN FACTS

Nickname: Big Bill
Occupations before being president: lawyer, judge, governor, secretary of war
Favorite foods: turtle soup
Pets: a cow named Pauline Wayne (the last to graze on the White House lawn)

WHAT WAS HAPPENING:

- Admiral Robert E. Peary discovered the North Pole.
- The *Titanic* struck an iceberg and sank.
- The U.S. population was about 97,200,000.
- There were forty-six stars on the flag.

Woodrow Wilson

PRESIDENT NUMBER: 28
YEARS HE WAS PRESIDENT: 1913-1921
FIRST LADY: ELLEN WILSON (SHE DIED
DURING HIS PRESIDENCY); EDITH WILSON

Wilson's picture is on the $100,000 bill, which is no longer in circulation.

He was the first president to hold a press conference.

His second wife, Edith Wilson, was the first woman in Washington to drive her own car.

THAT'S A LOT OF PIZZAS!

DOES DRIVING ONE OF THESE COUNT?

FUN FACTS

Nickname: Professor
Occupations before being president: lawyer, professor, writer, college president, governor
Hobbies or sports: golf, horseback riding, swimming
Pets: sheep that grazed on the White House lawn (one named Old Ike)

WHAT WAS HAPPENING:

- World War I raged for five years.
- The first commercial radio broadcasts were made.
- The U.S. population was about 108,600,000.
- There were forty-eight stars on the flag.

Warren G. Harding

PRESIDENT NUMBER: 29
YEARS HE WAS PRESIDENT: 1921-1923
FIRST LADY: FLORENCE HARDING

THEN HE WAS THE FIRST PRESIDENT TO SAY, "BRRRRRRRR!"

Harding was the first president to visit the territory of Alaska.

He was the first president to broadcast a speech on the radio.

Harding died in office. The exact cause is still unknown. Many believe he may have caught pneumonia.

CHECK OUT MY POKER FACE!

He played poker with his cabinet members.

During one of his poker games, Harding gambled away a complete set of White House china.

FUN FACTS

Nickname: Wobbly Warren

Occupations before being president: journalist, newspaper owner, lieutenant governor, senator

Favorite foods: cabbage, sauerkraut, sausage

Hobbies or sports: golf, horseback riding

Pets: an Airedale named Laddie Boy, an English bulldog named Old Boy

WHAT WAS HAPPENING:

- The U.S.S.R. was formed.
- The first hearing aids were developed.
- The U.S. population was about 111,900,000.
- There were forty-eight stars on the flag.

Calvin Coolidge

PRESIDENT NUMBER: 30
YEARS HE WAS PRESIDENT: 1923-1929
FIRST LADY: GRACE COOLIDGE

Coolidge had an electric horse installed in the White House that he rode almost daily, whooping like a cowboy.

YEE-HAW!

Coolidge didn't talk much. A woman once bet him that she could make him say more than three words. He replied, "You lose," and won the bet.

He enjoyed afternoon naps and supposedly slept more hours in a day than any other president.

Coolidge was a practical joker. Sometimes he would press all the buttons on his desk, then laugh as all his aides appeared at his office door at once.

FUN FACTS

Nickname: Silent Cal
Occupations before being president: lawyer, state legislator, mayor, governor, vice president
Hobbies or sports: fishing, golf, trapshooting, riding his mechanical horse

WHAT WAS HAPPENING:

- The first "talking" motion picture was produced— *The Jazz Singer*.
- Charles Lindbergh flew nonstop across the Atlantic Ocean.
- Walt Disney produced the first cartoon with sound.
- The U.S. population was about 122,000,000.
- There were forty-eight stars on the flag.

Herbert Hoover

PRESIDENT NUMBER: 31
YEARS HE WAS PRESIDENT: 1929-1933
FIRST LADY: LOU HOOVER

Hoover was the first president to have a telephone on his desk.

Mrs. Hoover spoke several different languages.

Every morning, before breakfast, Hoover exercised—in rain, shine, or snow.

Mrs. Hoover once served as president of the Girl Scouts.

He was the first president to have an asteroid named after him.

FUN FACTS

Nickname: Chief
Occupations before being president: engineer, businessman, food relief administrator, secretary of commerce
Favorite foods: sweet potatoes with roasted marshmallows
Hobbies or sports: fly-fishing
Pets: a dog named King Tut, other dogs

WHAT WAS HAPPENING:

- The stock market crashed, beginning the Great Depression.
- The ballpoint pen was introduced in the United States.
- The U.S. population was about 125,600,000.
- There were forty-eight stars on the flag.

Franklin Delano Roosevelt

PRESIDENT NUMBER: 32

YEARS HE WAS PRESIDENT: 1933-1945

FIRST LADY: ELEANOR ROOSEVELT

I'LL WATCH ANYTHING AS LONG AS I HAVE PLENTY OF POPCORN

Confined to a wheelchair because of polio, Franklin Roosevelt spent hours practicing crawling out of a room in case he had to face a fire alone.

He was the first president to deliver a speech on television.

The American people broke with tradition and elected Roosevelt to third and fourth terms as president.

His stamp collection sold for more than $200,000 after he died.

He was the cousin of former president Theodore Roosevelt.

I HAVE A FOOD COLLECTION

FUN FACTS

Nickname: FDR

Occupations before being president: lawyer, state senator, assistant secretary of the navy, business executive, governor

Favorite foods: pancakes, fish, cabbage, sweet potatoes

Hobbies or sports: sailing, swimming, collecting miniature pigs

Pets: a Scottish terrier named Fala, a German shepherd named Major

WHAT WAS HAPPENING:

- World War II began.
- Japan attacked the United States at Pearl Harbor.
- A radio show about a fictional alien invasion, "War of the Worlds," caused thousands to panic.
- The U.S. population was about 140,000,000.
- There were forty-eight stars on the flag.

Harry S. Truman

PRESIDENT NUMBER: 33
YEARS HE WAS PRESIDENT: 1945-1953
FIRST LADY: BESS TRUMAN

Truman's closets were notoriously messy.

He had nine clocks in his office.

He had read every book in his local library by age fifteen.

He personally designed the current presidential seal.

Truman's daughter, Margaret, is a bestselling author of mystery novels.

Truman was the first president to travel underwater in a modern submarine.

FUN FACTS

Nickname: Man from Independence

Occupations before being president: bank clerk, farmer, soldier, businessman, judge, senator, vice president

Favorite foods: angel food cake, peach cobbler

Hobbies or sports: piano, swimming, wrestling, walking, reading

Pets: an Irish setter named Mike

WHAT WAS HAPPENING:

• World War II ended.
• The Korean War began.
• Edwin Land invented the Polaroid camera.
• Americans saw the first nationwide television show.
• The U.S. population was about 159,700,000.
• There were forty-eight stars on the flag.

Dwight D. Eisenhower

PRESIDENT NUMBER: 34
YEARS HE WAS PRESIDENT: 1953-1961
FIRST LADY: MAMIE EISENHOWER

Eisenhower didn't drive, didn't know how to use a telephone, and didn't handle money.

He was the first president to appear on color TV.

He was the first president to have a pilot's license.

He named the presidential retreat Camp David after his grandson.

He had a putting green installed on the White House lawn.

Eisenhower once played minor league baseball.

STILL VERY RELAXING

FUN FACTS

Nickname: Ike

Occupations before being president: soldier, supreme commander of the Allied forces in World War II, college president, NATO commander

Favorite foods: steak, vegetable soup, prune whip dessert

Hobbies or sports: bridge, fishing, golf, painting, cooking

Pets: a Weimaraner named Heidi

WHAT WAS HAPPENING:

- The Korean War ended.
- The Soviet Union launched the first satellite, *Sputnik 1*.
- The U.S. population was about 181,700,000.
- There were now fifty stars on the flag. And that's the same as it is today!

John F. Kennedy

PRESIDENT NUMBER: 35
YEARS HE WAS PRESIDENT: 1961-1963
FIRST LADY: JACQUELINE KENNEDY

Kennedy had not even served half his term when he was tragically shot in Texas. Though Lee Harvey Oswald was arrested for the murder, some still believe the case has not really been solved.

Kennedy used a sunlamp daily in order to get his healthy "glow."

He once hired a drama coach to help him with public speaking. One of the exercises had him barking for two minutes straight.

One of his legs was shorter than the other.

He was the first Boy Scout to become president.

FASHION ALERT: Kennedy was the first president not to wear a hat.

FUN FACTS

Nicknames: JFK, Jack
Occupations before being president: author, naval officer, journalist, congressman, senator
Favorite foods: New England clam chowder
Hobbies or sports: sailing, swimming, football
Pets: rabbits, hamsters, birds, cats, a pony named Macaroni, dogs

WHAT WAS HAPPENING:

- Yuri Gagarin became the first person in space.
- John Glenn Jr. became the first American to orbit Earth.
- The U.S. population was about 190,417,800.

Lyndon B. Johnson

PRESIDENT NUMBER: 36
YEARS HE WAS PRESIDENT: 1963-1969
FIRST LADY: LYNDA "LADY BIRD" JOHNSON

Johnson's parents didn't name him until three months after he was born.

He would often roam the White House, turning off unused lights.

NOW THAT'S CHANNEL SURFING IN STYLE!

CLICK CLICK CLICK CLICK CLICK

Johnson had phones installed everywhere—in his cars, boats, planes, and swimming pools (on floating rafts).

He had three television sets in his bedroom. That way he could watch all three major networks at once.

He was the first president to be sworn in by a woman.

Johnson gave away electric toothbrushes as gifts. That way, whenever someone brushed their teeth, they would think of him.

FUN FACTS

Nickname: LBJ
Occupations before being president: teacher, rancher, congressman, senator, vice president
Favorite foods: seafood, chipped beef, chili, barbecued ribs
Hobbies or sports: fishing, hunting, horseback riding
Pets: beagles named Him and Her, a dog named Yuki

WHAT WAS HAPPENING:

- The Vietnam conflict grew into a full-scale war.
- The first successful human heart transplant was performed.
- The U.S. population was about 205,000,000.

Richard M. Nixon

PRESIDENT NUMBER: 37
YEARS HE WAS PRESIDENT: 1969-1974
FIRST LADY: PAT NIXON

HOW BIG WERE HIS PHONE BILLS?

Nixon was the first president to visit all fifty states.

He gave singer Elvis Presley a badge and enlisted him in the war against drugs.

When Nixon couldn't sleep, he would call friends and staff. One night he made fifty calls.

GLAD HE DIDN'T HAVE MY NUMBER

He was the only president to resign from office (due to the Watergate scandal).

He often became tangled in the leash when he walked his dogs.

He was the only president to place a telephone call to the moon. This happened when he congratulated the astronauts of *Apollo 11* on their moon landing.

FUN FACTS

Nickname: Tricky Dick

Occupations before being president: lawyer, naval officer, congressman, senator, vice president

Hobbies or sports: bowling, golf, piano

Pets: dogs named Vicky, Pasha, and King Timahoe

WHAT WAS HAPPENING:

- Neil Armstrong and Edwin "Buzz" Aldrin Jr. became the first people to set foot on the moon.
- The U.S. withdrew most of its forces from South Vietnam.
- The U.S. population was about 213,235,298.

Gerald R. Ford

PRESIDENT NUMBER: 38
YEARS HE WAS PRESIDENT: 1974-1977
FIRST LADY: BETTY FORD

To earn extra money in law school, Gerald Ford was a fashion model.

. . . AND I SAID, "WE'RE NOT MEETING IN THE CABINET, WE'RE HAVING A CABINET MEETING!"

He was the only president to have been an Eagle Scout.

He was the only president to have been recruited by the National Football League.

His daughter, Susan, held her senior prom in the White House.

He and Mrs. Ford had pillow fights.

After state dinners, Ford would sometimes stay up until one o'clock in the morning dancing to rock music.

He was right-handed when standing up (for sports) and left-handed when sitting (eating and writing).

Ford was the first president to hire someone who just wrote jokes.

FUN FACTS

Nickname: Mr. Nice Guy
Occupations before being president: football coach, lawyer, naval officer, congressman, vice president
Favorite foods: strawberries
Hobbies or sports: golf, jogging, sailing, swimming, skiing
Pets: a golden retriever named Liberty, a Siamese cat named Shan

WHAT WAS HAPPENING:

- The Vietnam War ended.
- The unmanned *Viking I* became the first U.S. spacecraft to land on Mars.
- The U.S. population was about 220,000,000.

James E. Carter

PRESIDENT NUMBER: 39
YEARS HE WAS PRESIDENT: 1977-1981
FIRST LADY: ROSALYNN CARTER

I'LL PLAY AS LONG AS I GET LASAGNA LATER

Carter ordered all White House thermostats to be turned down in order to save energy.

He was informal. He even told Secret Service agents to stop opening doors for him.

The First Family enjoyed throwing Frisbees on the White House lawn.

He was a former officer on a submarine.

He had a lucky red tie.

Believe it or not, Jimmy Carter was the first president to be born in a hospital and not at home.

FUN FACTS

Nickname: Jimmy
Occupations before being president: naval officer, peanut farmer, state senator, governor
Favorite foods: peanut soup, lentil-and-franks soup, corn bread
Hobbies or sports: canoeing, fishing, jogging, skiing, softball, tennis, swimming
Pets: a dog named Grits, a Siamese cat named Misty Malarky Ying Yang

WHAT WAS HAPPENING:

- The Three Mile Island nuclear accident occurred.
- Most states rationed gasoline due to high oil prices.
- The U.S. population was about 224,226,000.

Ronald Reagan

PRESIDENT NUMBER: 40
YEARS HE WAS PRESIDENT: 1981-1989
FIRST LADY: NANCY REAGAN

Reagan was sixty-nine when he was elected, making him the oldest president in history.

I'M AN ACTOR. MAYBE I SHOULD RUN FOR PRESIDENT

He was the first professional movie actor to become president.

He wore a smaller shirt collar so his head didn't look too big for his body (a trick he'd learned from his days in Hollywood).

He rescued seventy-seven people when he was a young lifeguard.

He was the first president to have been divorced.

He once was a baseball announcer.

FUN FACTS

Nickname: Dutch
Occupations before being president: radio announcer, actor, union president, governor
Favorite foods: jelly beans, popcorn, Mexican food
Hobbies or sports: swimming, horseback riding
Pets: a King Charles Cavalier spaniel named Rex, dogs and horses at his ranch

WHAT WAS HAPPENING:

• The space shuttle *Columbia*, the first reusable spacecraft, was launched.
• The IBM PC computer was invented.
• The Apple Macintosh computer was invented.
• The U.S. population was about 247,498,000.

George H.W. Bush

PRESIDENT NUMBER: 41
YEARS HE WAS PRESIDENT: 1989-1993
FIRST LADY: BARBARA BUSH

Bush was an All-American baseball player in college.

He was the first president to publicly refuse to eat broccoli.

Both of his family dogs had books published—*Millie's Book* and *C. Fred's Story*.

At nineteen, he was one of the youngest combat pilots in the navy.

I'M PUBLICLY REFUSING TO SHARE. BACK AWAY FROM THE PIZZA

FUN FACTS

Nickname: Poppy

Occupations before being president: navy pilot, businessman, congressman, UN ambassador, CIA director, vice president

Favorite foods: Chinese food, pork rinds smothered in Tabasco sauce

Hobbies or sports: boating, fishing, golf, horseshoes, jogging, tennis

Pets: two English Springer spaniels named Millie and Ranger

WHAT WAS HAPPENING:

- The Berlin Wall fell.
- The Persian Gulf War began and ended.
- The Soviet Union dissolved.
- The U.S. population at the time was about 256,300,000.

45

William J. Clinton

PRESIDENT NUMBER: 42
YEARS HE WAS PRESIDENT: 1993-2001
FIRST LADY: HILLARY RODHAM CLINTON

Clinton has collected books about the lives of presidents since he was a boy.

When he was thirty-two, he was the youngest governor in the country.

He had chronic laryngitis from allergies and overusing his voice.

He was the second president to be impeached.

He turned down several music scholarships after he graduated from high school.

He once worked as a Red Cross volunteer.

When he was sixteen, Clinton met President Kennedy. The meeting inspired Clinton to go into politics.

MAYBE HE'LL BUY THIS ONE!

FUN FACTS

Nickname: Bill, The Man from Hope
Occupations before being president: lawyer, law professor, state attorney general, governor
Favorite foods: bananas spread with peanut butter, tacos, mango ice cream
Hobbies or sports: golf, jogging, reading, football, playing the saxophone
Pets: a chocolate Labrador named Buddy, a cat named Socks

WHAT WAS HAPPENING:

- NASA's *Pathfinder* spacecraft landed on Mars and transmitted television images.
- The first clone of an adult mammal, a sheep named Dolly, was born in Scotland.
- The U.S. population was about 275,119,000.

George W. Bush

PRESIDENT NUMBER: 43
YEARS HE WAS PRESIDENT: 2001-2005
FIRST LADY: LAURA BUSH

Bush was the first president to deliver the same radio address from the Oval Office in English and Spanish.

He was the second president to be the son of a former president.

He was the only president to have played Little League baseball when he was younger, and he sometimes hosted a T-ball game for young guests at the White House.

His dog Spot was born in the White House, making him the only second-generation presidential pet.

He was the first president to have twins.

When he was a boy, he didn't dream of being president. He dreamed of being Willie Mays—a famous baseball player at the time.

He was the first to give a video tour of the White House over the Internet.

FUN FACTS

Nickname: Dubya
Occupations before being president: businessman, owner of a Major League Baseball team, governor
Favorite foods: Mexican food
Pets: an English springer spaniel named Spot, a Scottish terrier named Barney, a cat named India, and a longhorn cow named Ofelia (at his ranch)

WHAT WAS HAPPENING:

- Terrorists attacked the United States on September 11, 2001.
- The U.S. war with Iraq began.
- The U.S. population was about 285,500,000.

So there you have it—a bunch of funny quirks, fascinating facts, and sometimes unusual habits of our forty-three presidents. Just goes to show that all presidents are human. Which means that you, too, could someday be the leader of our country. Just do me a favor—when you get to the White House, have them install a pet door. That way I can come visit.

If you want to learn more about the presidents, head to your local library or bookstore. You can get the scoop on just about anything in a good book.

Maybe I'll do some research of my own. Why, I might even become president someday! Then again, it sounds like too much work. I think I'll settle for secretary of food or maybe chairman of the napping committee.

GARFIELD

Bibliography

Barber, James. *Presidents*. New York: DK Publishing, 2000.

Humes, James. *Which President Killed a Man?* New York: McGraw-Hill, 2003.

Krull, Kathleen. *Lives of the Presidents*. Orlando: Harcourt Brace & Company, 1998.

Pitch, Anthony S. *Exclusively Presidential Trivia*. Potomac: Mino Publications, 2001.

"Presidents and First Ladies." *The White House Official Website*. March 1, 2004 <www.whitehouse.gov>.

Rubel, David. *The Scholastic Encyclopedia of the Presidents and Their Times*. New York: Scholastic Reference, 2001.

The World Book of America's Presidents. Chicago: World Book, 2002.